$30.95 Nov/03 Apple Media
Smart

MT.  IDARY

MW01224882

The Earth and Its Moon

RUTH ASHBY

Published by Smart Apple Media, 1980 Lookout Drive, North Mankato, Minnesota 56003

Photo Credits: Page 4, 7, 8: courtesy NASA. Page 9: copyright © 2003 William K. Hartmann. Page 11: courtesy NASA. Page 12: copyright © 2003 Calvin J. Hamilton. Page 13: copyright © 2003 ZoomSchool.com. Page 15: courtesy NASA. Page 16: copyright © 2003 Dr. Steven Daunt. Page 18, 20: courtesy NASA. Page 21: copyright © 2003 Calvin J. Hamilton. Page 22, 23, 24: courtesy NASA. Page 27: courtesy United States Naval Observatory. Page 29: copyright © 2003 Fred Espenak. Page 30, 31, 32 (top), 32 (bottom), 33, 35, 36, 37, 38, 40: courtesy NASA. Page 42-45: courtesy United States Naval Observatory.
Cover art courtesy NASA.

Library of Congress Cataloging-in-Publication Data

Ashby, Ruth.
The Earth and its moon / by Ruth Ashby.
p. cm. — (The new solar system)
Summary: A discussion of the origins and physical characteristics of the earth and its moon, voyages to the moon, and the study of the earth from space.
ISBN 1-58340-287-X
1. Earth—Juvenile literature. 2. Moon—Juvenile literature. [1. Earth. 2. Moon.] I. Title. II. Series.
QB631.4.A84 2003   525—dc21   2003042753

First Edition

9 8 7 6 5 4 3 2 1

Contents

Earth rises above the Moon's horizon in this famous picture taken by the *Apollo 8* astronauts in 1968.

4

From Earth to the Moon

On Christmas Eve, 1968, the astronauts of the *Apollo 8* mission, the first humans to orbit the Moon, saw a breathtaking sight: Earth rising above the Moon. Thinking fast, astronaut Bill Anders grabbed a nearby camera and shot a color photograph of the astonishing scene. This image became the first widely circulated color photograph of the planet Earth as seen from the Moon. In it, Earth, a luminous blue and white ball set against the darkness of space, floats over the barren lunar landscape.

The now-famous picture shows our home planet in a new light. As Anders's fellow astronaut Jim Lovell said, Earth is "a grand oasis in the big vastness of space." As the photograph emphasizes, Earth is also forever linked to the Moon, its only satellite. For millennia, humans have watched moonrise from the surface of Earth. Now we have seen earthrise over the horizon of the Moon.

Earth and its Moon are the only two heavenly bodies that humans have explored in person and are the two we know best. Yet we are continually learning more about them and being astonished by what we discover. The second half of the 20th century witnessed an incredible explosion of knowledge about our solar system and the universe. In that time, humans used probes to explore the planets, telescopes to search the stars, and sent astronauts to walk on the Moon. In this book we will review some of the astonishing things we've found out about Earth and the Moon in the last 50 years. In the next 50, we will learn even more.

To begin, let's review a few basic facts. Earth is the third planet from a medium-sized star called the Sun, which it orbits at an average distance of approximately 93 million miles (150 million km). The fifth-largest planet in our solar system, the Earth makes one complete revolution around the Sun every $365\frac{1}{4}$ days, or one year. Every 23 hours and 56 minutes, it makes one complete rotation, or turn, on its axis. Its axis is oblique, with a tilt of 23.5 degrees from the vertical. Therefore, the Sun is shining almost directly on the southern hemisphere for six months of the year and on the northern hemisphere for six months. This axial tilt determines our four seasons: spring, summer, fall, and winter.

Earth is unique in many ways. It is the only planet in the solar system where the average temperature is between the boiling and freezing points of water. As a result, it is the only planet with liquid water on its surface. It also is the only planet with an atmosphere containing breathable oxygen, and as far as we know, the only planet that has living things.

Earth has one natural satellite: the Moon. About 239,000 miles (384,500 km) from Earth, it is 2,160 miles (3,476 km) in diameter, about one-quarter of the size of Earth. It has no liquid water on its surface, no atmosphere, and no life. The Moon is, in the words of astronaut Edwin "Buzz" Aldrin, a place of "magnificent desolation."

A comet speeds towards the Sun in this artist's conception of our solar system's inner planets. The lines around the planets indicate the path of their orbits and the orbits of the Moon and the moons of Mars.

This famous photograph of Earth was taken on December 7, 1972, by the crew of *Apollo 17* as they were traveling toward the Moon.

Earth: The Grand Oasis

Imagine a planet where the surface is covered with oceans of hot lava, the atmosphere is a dense stew of carbon dioxide and water vapor, and rocks fall like rain from the sky. Is this a place you would like to call home? Probably not. But that is what Earth was like more than four billion years ago.

Earth came violently to life 4.5 billion years ago in a remote corner of the Milky Way galaxy. Its birthplace was a swirling disk of dust and gas around a young star we now call the Sun. As the dust orbited, particles began to stick together to form small rocky masses called planetesimals, which crashed into each other and grew larger. The more massive they grew, the greater their gravitational pull, and the more violent the collisions became. Eventually, the largest of the pieces of debris turned into planets, and the smaller bits became meteorites. Our solar system was born.

Less than a million years after the Sun formed, the solar system was a swirling disk of dust and gases. This illustration shows small grains of dust before they combined into planetesimals in the region of the future Earth.

The inner rocky planets are Mercury, Venus, Earth, and Mars. Further out are the gas giants: Jupiter, Saturn, Uranus, and Neptune. When the planets formed, they probably had dense hydrogen atmospheres. But the early Sun went through a stormy period during which the solar wind—a steady stream of fast-moving particles—probably blew off the gas envelopes of the inner planets, pushing the hydrogen toward the outer regions, where the far planets could have gravitationally attracted it.

In the first hundreds of millions of years of Earth's existence, it was pounded continually by planetesimals that generated a lot of heat. The heat melted the surface into an ocean of thick, boiling lava. Heavier elements, such as iron and nickel, sank toward the center of the molten planet, while lighter elements, such as silicon and aluminum, moved to the outer layers. Flying comets and meteorites pockmarked the planet with craters. Fiery volcanoes spewed lava, dust, and gases into the primitive atmosphere. The young Earth was as barren and battered as today's Moon and as scorching hot as Venus.

How did Earth transform from the deadly inferno of its early existence into the life-giving oasis of today? No one is exactly sure. Scientists do agree on some basics, however.

During the era of meteor bombardment, about 4.5 to 3.8 billion years ago, volcanoes on Earth spewed carbon dioxide and water vapor into the thin but growing atmosphere. When the water vapor reached colder altitudes, it condensed into water droplets that rained back on Earth, cooling the young planet. As the temperature dropped, the water began to pool into craters to form the first lakes and oceans. By the time Earth was two billion years old, most of it was covered with water. Today, oceans cover 70 percent of its surface.

It was in these abundant oceans that the first unicellular organisms appeared. About 3.5 billion years ago, blue-green algae developed the capability of making their own food by using the Sun's energy to break down carbon dioxide and minerals. This primitive photosynthesis produced oxygen, which slowly began to enter the atmosphere. Over the next billion years, the percentage of oxygen

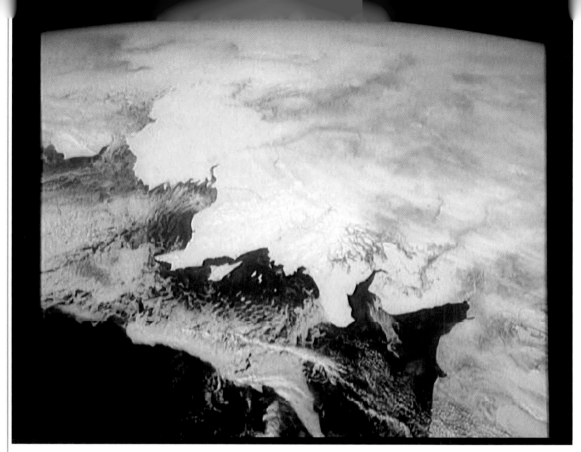

Earth is the only planet in the solar system where three forms of water—solid (ice), liquid (ocean), and gas (water vapor in clouds)—exist simultaneously. This view of Earth from space, looking north to the Bering Sea and the coast of Alaska, shows water in all three states.

in the atmosphere increased until it reached 21 percent, about where it is today. Carbon dioxide, though, decreased to almost nothing.

Meanwhile, Earth continued to cool and develop its present structure. Like the other planets, it is nearly round, although it bulges just a bit at the equator. It is composed of three major layers: the core, the mantle, and the outer shell, or crust. Together, they are estimated to weigh more than six billion trillion tons (6×10^{21} t).

At the center of Earth is the inner core. About the size of the Moon, it is composed primarily of solid iron and nickel. Although the inner core may be as hot as the surface of the Sun—about 11,000°F (6,000°C)—the pressure at the center of Earth is so intense that the "metal ball" remains solid.

The outer core, though, is molten. Here, spinning metallic liquid produces the electrical currents that create Earth's magnetic field. Our magnetic field runs north-south, which can easily be observed with a compass. William Gilbert (1544–1603), Queen Elizabeth I's physician and a great scientist, was the first to point out that Earth might be magnetic. Once in a great while—about six times in the last million years—the field has reversed, so that the north pole became the south pole, and vice versa. No one is quite sure why this happens.

The magnetic field is useful for more than just enabling us to find directions when we travel. It also forms a kind of shield around Earth, called the magnetosphere, that protects us from the charged particles—mostly electrons and protons—that stream out from the Sun. Without protection from the solar wind, we would fry in a stream of radiation.

Above the outer core lies the mantle, the thickest layer of the planet. It makes up 83 percent of Earth's total volume and 67 percent of its mass. The lower mantle, made of semiliquid rocks composed of magnesium, iron, and silicon,

This cutaway view shows the major regions of Earth's interior. Starting from the surface we see the crust (the thin outer layer), the mantle, the liquid outer core, and the solid inner core. Geologists learn about the center of Earth by studying seismic (shock) waves during earthquakes. Scientists can measure when waves bend or slow down as they travel through different layers of rock.

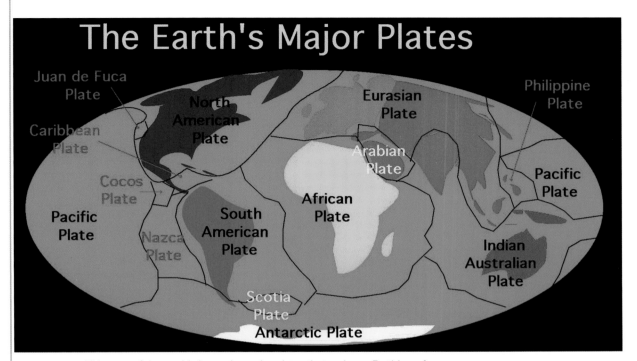

The Earth's Major Plates

Juan de Fuca Plate

Caribbean Plate

Cocos Plate

Pacific Plate

Nazca Plate

North American Plate

South American Plate

Scotia Plate

Eurasian Plate

Arabian Plate

African Plate

Philippine Plate

Pacific Plate

Indian Australian Plate

Antarctic Plate

This map of the world shows the major plates that make up Earth's surface.

extends from 400 to 1,800 miles (650–2,890 km) into the center. The more solid upper mantle is covered by a thin crust of rock on the surface. This crust is thickest on the continents. The continental crust averages about 25 miles (40 km) deep, but the oceanic crust is only about 6 miles (9.6 km) deep. The crust and the most rigid part of the upper mantle make up the lithosphere, which can reach a depth of from 186 to 250 miles (300–400 km) beneath the surface.

For centuries, scientists believed that since the lithosphere was solid rock, the crust of Earth did not move. But in 1912, a German scientist named Alfred Wegener proposed an astounding theory. He suggested that our continents had shifted over hundreds of thousands of years. When the dinosaurs first appeared some 245 million years ago, the continents were joined together in one supercontinent Wegener called "Pangea." Since then, the continents have drifted apart.

How could this have happened?

For a long time, no one knew. Without firm evidence, other geologists were reluctant to support Wegener's theory. Not until the late 1960s did they understand how continental drift occurs. They discovered that the lithosphere is broken into more than 14 separate segments called plates that fit into each other like pieces in a jigsaw puzzle. These plates float around on top of the semimelted mantle beneath. Although the plates move only an estimated two to four inches (5–10 cm) per year, over millions of years, those inches add up. For example, the Atlantic Ocean is about 30 feet (9 m) wider now than when Columbus crossed it in 1492. As a result of plate tectonics, over time, continents have come together and split apart, mountains have risen up, oceans have been created, and volcanoes have erupted.

Most geologic activity—mountain formation, volcanic eruptions, and earthquakes—occurs at plate boundaries. Mountains are formed when two continental plates collide

The Ring of Fire

The largest of Earth's tectonic plates, the Pacific plate, covers one-fifth of Earth's surface and borders seven other plates. It moves slowly in a counterclockwise direction, about $2^{1}/_{2}$ inches (6 cm) a year. Wherever plates collide, geologic activity occurs. Earthquakes result where the Pacific plate slides past the North American plate along the California coast. But where the Pacific plate dives under the Indo-Australian, Eurasian, and Philippine plates, volcanoes erupt. Many of the world's major volcanoes are found along the edges of the Pacific plate, in Japan, Indonesia, the Philippines, New Zealand, Alaska, and North America. Geologists call the chain of volcanoes around the Pacific Ocean the "Ring of Fire."

The San Andreas Fault in California, one of the longest and most active faults in the world, is clearly visible to the right of the mountains in this exaggerated-height image. Along this fault, the Pacific plate and North American plate slip a few centimeters a year, causing an earthquake about once every 22 years. This image was created by combining a radar image from the space shuttle *Endeavor* with data from the *Landsat* satellite.

and fold upon each other. The Himalayas, for instance, were formed when the Indo-Australian plate collided with the Eurasian plate 35 million years ago.

Volcanoes are formed when a lighter continental plate hits a heavy oceanic plate. Because the ocean plate is denser, it is subducted, or slides down, into the mantle, and magma rises through the crust. Mount St. Helens, a volcano in Washington state that erupted violently in 1980, was formed on the line between the Pacific plate and the North American plate.

Earthquakes also occur when two plates clash, whether because one plate is subducted or because it grinds past the other. At the San Andreas Fault in California, two plates meet and slide past each other in different directions. This stress is what caused the great San Francisco earthquake of 1906.

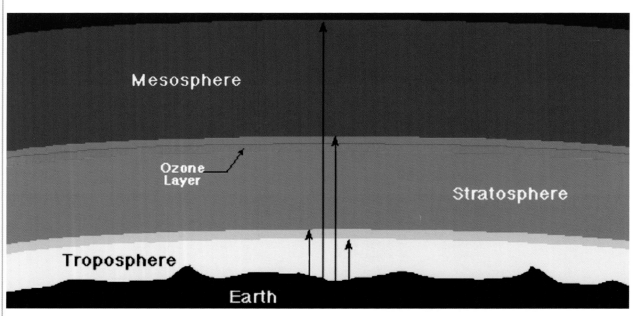

Earth's atmosphere extends up from the surface about 400 miles (650 km) into space. The two lower layers, the troposphere and the stratosphere, contain 99 percent of the air in Earth's atmosphere.

The surface of Earth is dynamic, ever renewing and ever changing. Earth is also set apart from other solar system planets by the cocoon of gas we call the atmosphere. The other planets are made up mostly of gases that were plentiful at the time of the solar system's creation: hydrogen, helium, methane, and ammonia. Only Earth has an atmosphere capable of sustaining life as we know it. The evolution of bacteria and plants has given it an atmosphere composed of approximately 78 percent nitrogen, 21 percent oxygen, 1 percent argon, 1 percent water vapor, and traces of carbon dioxide. Among the smaller terrestrial planets, only Earth and Venus have gravity strong enough to attract enough gas molecules to create a real atmosphere. And Venus's atmosphere is a lethal brew of mostly carbon dioxide plus sulphur dioxide.

Extending 400 miles (650 km) into space, Earth's atmosphere is composed of several protective layers. The lowest level, the moist and turbulent troposphere, contains all the clouds and weather. The troposphere is deeper at the equator (12 miles, or 18 km) than at the poles (5 miles, or 8 km). Its winds and ocean currents spread heat around the globe and keep the temperature relatively uniform and moderate. Here, gravity traps most of the atmosphere's air, which grows thinner at higher altitudes. Within the next level beyond, the stratosphere, 31 miles (50 km) high, lies the important ozone layer, which absorbs much of the Sun's damaging ultraviolet light. The upper layers—the mesosphere, 53 miles (85 km) high; the thermosphere, 300 miles (480 km) high; and the exosphere, 400 miles (650 km) high—also block the Sun's ultraviolet light and burn up most meteoroids before they can reach the surface of Earth.

Wrapped in a moist, warm blanket of air, Earth is insulated from space. It is hard to imagine what's beyond when we look up during the daytime and see the familiar blue sky and white clouds of our own troposphere. It is only at night, when the stars and Moon come out, that we see far beyond our own planet. The Moon is our closest link to the rest of the universe.

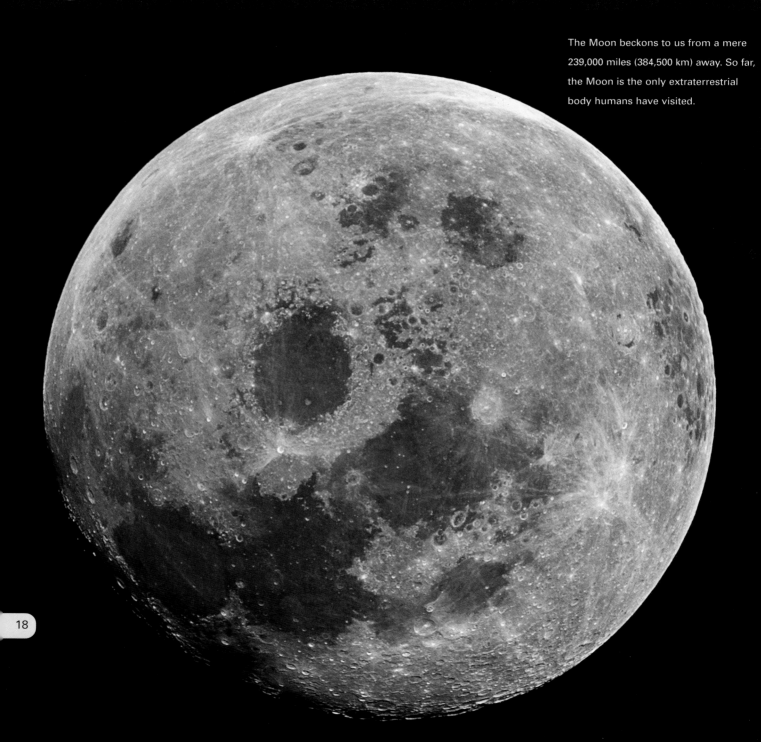

The Moon beckons to us from a mere 239,000 miles (384,500 km) away. So far, the Moon is the only extraterrestrial body humans have visited.

The Moon: A Barren World

Where did the Moon come from? Was it once part of Earth? Or was it an independent planet that floated into Earth's orbit? Astronomers have debated these questions for centuries. Three hypotheses, or theories, were popular before space exploration in the late 20th century called them all into question.

First came the nebular hypothesis proposed by astronomer Pierre Simon Laplace in 1796. He theorized that the Moon was formed with Earth as a double planet in the spinning gaseous cloud out of which the solar system was born. This theory was popular for a long time but was finally discarded on mathematical grounds.

The second hypothesis suggested that the Moon was thrown out of Earth in one great mass. The fission hypothesis, advanced in 1881 by George Darwin (the son of Charles Darwin, who developed the theory of evolution), supposed that the spinning Earth elongated in a dumbbell shape until the neck snapped and the Moon broke free. Later, astronomer W. H. Pickering took Darwin's theory further by marrying it to Wegener's theory of continental drift. He speculated that the Pacific Ocean was the huge hole left behind. But it is now known that the Pacific Ocean is too shallow to be the scar left by a body the size of the Moon. Scientists have also concluded that because of gravity it is physically impossible for a large mass to break out of a planet this way.

Perhaps the Moon was formed in a different part of the early solar system and was captured by the gravity of Earth. That was the basis of the third theory, the so-called capture hypothesis. It seemed possible too, until the Apollo missions allowed us to analyze lunar rocks for the first time. We have discovered that the composition of the Moon and the upper mantle of Earth are quite similar. That means they were formed in the same area of the original solar system dust cloud, not in different areas as the capture theory suggested.

The theory supported by most scientists today is the "giant-impact hypothesis." It proposes that about 4.5 billion years ago, the developing Earth was hit by a massive body as large as Mars. With the impact

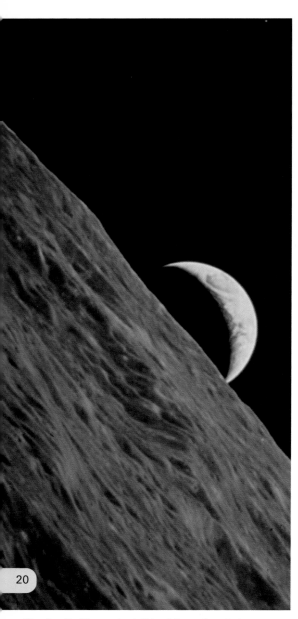

The *Apollo 17* crew took this picture of earthrise over the Moon as they were orbiting just a few dozen miles above the Moon.

of the collision, the mantles of both planets blew off and shot into space. The heavier iron core of the impactor may have fallen back to Earth, but the lighter crust and mantle went into orbit. Eventually, the material coalesced into one mass. This theory would explain why the Moon has a lower density than Earth and why its iron core, if it exists at all, is quite small. It would also explain why the Moon has few volatile, or unstable, substances with low boiling points, such as water. The volatiles would all have been vaporized by the heat of the impact.

The new, red-hot Moon was covered with a boiling ocean of magma, or molten rock. As the magma cooled, a rock crust formed on the lunar surface. Sometimes huge volcanic eruptions sent lava flowing across the surface, where it settled into impact craters left by meteors. Like Earth, the Moon was blasted by a massive meteoroid bombardment until about 3.8 billion years ago.

In time, the turbulence ceased. By about three billion years ago, the Moon would have looked essentially the same as it does today. That is because the Moon is geologically inert, meaning it has no active volcanoes and only small, barely noticeable moonquakes. And when quakes do occur, they do so 500 to 600 miles (800–960 km) below the surface and are so mild that they barely disturb the surface at all.

Also, the lunar crust is not broken into moving tectonic plates, as on Earth. As a result, the meteor craters that were blasted into its surface during the meteoroid bombardment have not changed their basic shape in three billion years.

Beneath the crust is a rock mantle, part of which may be molten. The core remains a mystery. We know that the Moon has almost no magnetic field, so its core is probably not super-heated molten iron. If a metal core does exist, it is solid and small, no more than 600 miles (960 km) across.

Although the Moon is about one-fourth the size of Earth, it has only a little more than one percent of the Earth's mass, because it is much less dense. That means its surface gravity is only about one-sixth that of Earth's, and it cannot retain an atmosphere. Without an atmosphere, the Moon's tempera-ture swings radically, from ⁻300°F (⁻184°C) at night to 214°F (101°C) at noon. Nor is its bar-ren surface protected from solar radiation or

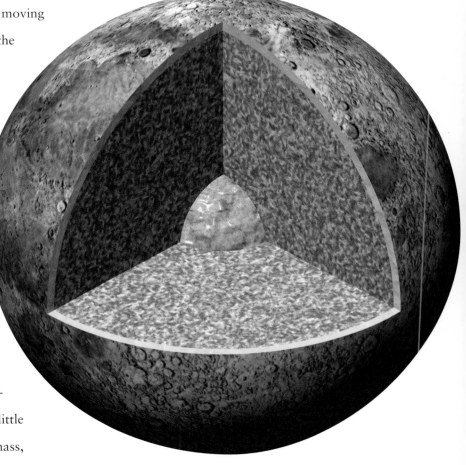

The Moon has a small, possibly metal, solid core, a large rock mantle, and a crust. Our knowledge of the lunar interior comes from measuring the seismic waves of moonquakes and from tracking spacecraft as they orbit the Moon. As spacecraft pass over regions of the Moon's crust, slight differences in gravitational pull cause the spacecraft to slow down or speed up. Scientists can then determine the thickness of the crust in a particular region.

meteorites. Anyone standing on the surface of the Moon would be exposed to the full force of the solar wind and a rain of micrometeorites. There, the sky is always black, and the world is silent.

The lunar landscape may be barren, but it is quite varied. Most of its features can be seen from Earth, even with the naked eye. These include:

- The maria (the Latin word for *seas*) are the dark plains areas. When the astronomer Galileo observed them with an early telescope in 1610, he thought they were bodies of water. Later they were found to be huge impact basins filled with basalt, which is hardened lava from volcanic eruptions. The maria make up about 16 percent of the Moon's surface.

- The terrae (the Latin word for *earth*) are the bright highland areas. Many are mountains that were formed at the edge of craters caused by meteor hits. Altogether, the highlands make up about 84 percent of the lunar surface.

- Craters are the bowl-shaped hollows made by meteors. Some terrae are made of chains of craters. There are thousands of craters on the Moon, some up to 200 miles (320 km) in diameter.

- Rays are bright streaks that emanate from craters for hundreds of miles or kilometers in every direction. They are made of glassy particles ejected when the craters formed.

- Regolith is the moon dust that covers the whole Moon. It results from the constant bombardment of lunar rocks by very small meteorites. Regolith may be as deep as 49 feet (15 m) in the highlands and 26 feet (8 m) in the lowlands.

The craters of the Moon are illuminated by reflected light from Earth—earth-shine—in this 1994 photograph taken by the orbiting *Clementine* spacecraft when it was a few thousand miles from the Moon. The Sun peeks over the lunar horizon as the planet Venus rises in the sky.

Apollo 17's lunar rover is dwarfed by a giant rock on the Moon's surface.

23

Separate images taken by the *Galileo* spacecraft were combined to create this collage of Earth and the Moon.

24

Partners in Space

Earth and the Moon have been companions for some 4.5 billion years and have always exerted a profound influence on each other. Consider that the Moon is responsible for our month. (The word *month* comes from the Old English word for *moon*.) Every 27 days, 7 hours, and 43 minutes, the Moon makes one orbit around Earth. This period of time is called the sidereal month. But as the Moon moves around Earth, Earth continues to orbit the Sun, so it takes the Moon an extra two days to catch up. By the time the Moon has again reached its initial position in our sky, $29\frac{1}{2}$ days have passed. This span is called the synodic month, or lunar month, and forms the basis for our month.

The Moon always has the same side turned toward Earth. This is not because it never turns on its axis, but because the time the Moon takes to rotate once is the exact time it takes to orbit Earth.

Is the synchronicity of the Moon's rotation and revolution a cosmic coincidence? No. Immediately after its formation, when the Moon was still red hot and semi-molten, the force of Earth's gravity caused the lunar rotation to slow down. Eventually Earth exerted such a strong pull on the near side of the Moon that it is turned toward Earth at all times.

But just because we always see one face of the Moon doesn't mean the Moon always looks the same. It appears to change shape in the course of every month, going from a crescent-shaped sliver to a glowing round sphere and back again. The Moon doesn't actually change form, of course. The variation results from the Sun's illumination of different portions of the Moon as it orbits around Earth. The different shapes the Moon appears to take during a month are called its phases.

The cycle begins with the new moon, when the Moon and the Sun are on the same side of Earth. The Sun lights up only the far side of the Moon, so the side facing us remains dark. As the Moon circles Earth, terrestrial observers can see the Sun shine on more and more of its surface. First comes the waxing (growing) crescent, then the first quarter half-moon, then the gibbous (Latin for "humpbacked") moon. At full moon, Earth is between the Sun and the Moon, and the Sun's light brightens the whole near side of the Moon. Then, as the Moon completes its revolution, we see less of it lit up. The phases progress through the waning (decreasing) gibbous Moon, the third quarter half-moon, and the waning crescent. The Moon has made a full circle around Earth and is dark once again.

You might wonder why the new moon doesn't completely obstruct our view of the Sun. In fact, sometimes it does, but not every month because the Moon's orbit is not on the same plane as Earth's. Two to five times a year, the Moon does pass in front of the Sun, and we have a solar eclipse. During a total solar eclipse, the Sun is blocked completely. All that is visible is a black disk surrounded by a halo of bright light called the corona. Because the Moon casts such a small shadow, a total solar eclipse is visible in one location on average only once every 350 years and only for a few minutes. In 2017, one will be visible in North America.

It might seem strange that the gigantic Sun could be completely blocked by such a small satellite. After all, the Sun's diameter is about 400 times that of the Moon. But it so happens that the Sun is also about 400 times farther away from Earth than the Moon is, so to a terrestrial observer, the Sun and the Moon look as if they're the same size. Now, that's a real cosmic coincidence!

Up to three times a year, the Moon passes into Earth's shadow. This event is called a lunar eclipse. During a lunar eclipse, Earth passes between the Moon and the Sun and all three are aligned. Because Earth's shadow is so much larger than the Moon's, lunar eclipses can be seen from more than half the Earth at one time. They also last much longer than solar eclipses—about three and a half hours.

Each month we see the Moon's appearance change. Throughout its cycles, the moon ranges from total darkness to full illumination depending upon its relationship to the Sun. From top left to bottom right, the lunar phases are waxing crescent, first-quarter half moon, waxing gibbous, full moon, waning gibbous, half moon, waning crescent, and new moon.

27

The Moon and Earth are so close to each other that they exert a mutual gravitational attraction called a tidal force. As mentioned, this force has slowed down the Moon's rotation so that there is a permanent "tug" on the side facing Earth. On Earth, this attraction causes the oceanic tides. The Moon pulls at the water on the side of Earth closest to it, causing the water to rise and fall twice a day. And on the opposite side of Earth, the water also bulges outward in a high tide. This happens because the Moon pulls Earth toward it and away from the water. High tides occur every 12 hours and 25 minutes—half the time between one moonrise and the next.

The size of the tides changes, depending in part upon how close Earth is to the Moon. At new moon or full moon, when the Moon and Sun are in line with each other, the tidal force is particularly strong and causes the spring tides, the highest tides of the month. The lowest tides, neap tides, occur when the Sun and Moon are at right angles and their gravitational pulls work against each other.

The Moon has one more amazing effect on Earth. Recently, scientists have decided that the Moon plays an important role in Earth's livability. Remember, Earth tilts 23.5 degrees on its axis, so one pole is always closer to the Sun. The Moon helps to stabilize this tilt. If it weren't for the Moon, the giant outer planets would exert so much gravitational force on Earth that it would wobble on its axis between 0 and 80 degrees. The extreme climate changes that would result would probably make Earth uninhabitable.

It is possible, then, that we owe our very existence to the Moon.

Leap Seconds

Did you know that Earth is slowing down? The tides actually act as giant brakes on Earth's rotation. On average, Earth is slowing down roughly 1.4 milliseconds per day, amounting to almost one second per year. In order to make sure that our global time scale, or Coordinated Universal Time (CUT), is synchronized with the rotation of Earth, extra seconds called "leap seconds" have to be added. Since 1972, 22 leap seconds have been added onto the last day of some Decembers and Junes. On December 31, 1998, for instance, New Year's Eve was longer than usual. The last minute of the year lasted 61 seconds!

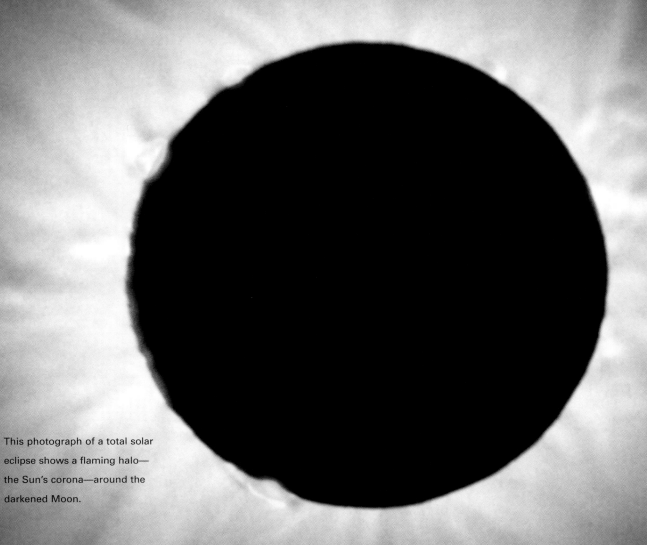

This photograph of a total solar eclipse shows a flaming halo—the Sun's corona—around the darkened Moon.

Apollo 11 astronaut Neil Armstrong took this famous picture of Edwin "Buzz" Aldrin standing on the Moon in July 1969. Armstrong and the lunar module *Eagle* are reflected in Aldrin's transparent helmet.

Exploring Earth and the Moon from Space

Humans have long dreamed of going to the Moon. But we didn't develop the technology that made it possible until the late 1950s. On May 25, 1961, President John F. Kennedy told the United States Congress, "I believe that this nation should commit itself to achieving the goal, before this decade is out, of landing a man on the Moon and returning him safely to Earth." But before 1961, no human being had even orbited Earth. How could this dream come true in less than 10 years?

The race to explore space began in 1957, when the Soviets launched the world's first artificial satellite, *Sputnik I*. The Soviet Union maintained its lead for the next few years. In 1959, they sent three probes to the Moon. The first was a flyby; the second crashlanded; and the third, *Luna 3*, took the first pictures of the far side of the Moon. These pictures showed that it was far less varied than the near side, with fewer maria and a thicker crust. Then, in 1961, Soviet cosmonaut Yuri Gagarin became the first person in orbit—for 108 minutes—and it seemed the Soviets might win the space race. But less than a month later, Alan

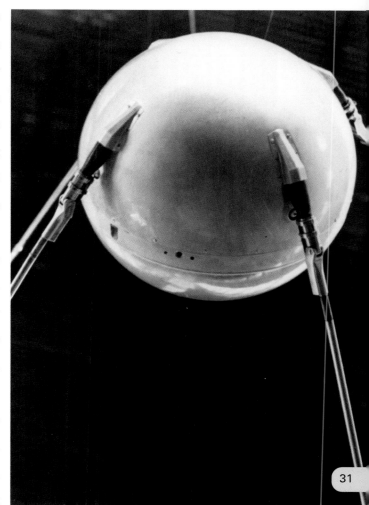

The spidery *Sputnik* satellite, launched by the Soviet Union in October 1957, was the first artificial object to orbit Earth. *Sputnik* means "traveling companion" in Russian.

The *Apollo 8* crew, the first humans to orbit the Moon, pose on a Kennedy Space Center simulator in their space suits. From left to right are James A. Lovell Jr., William A. Anders, and Frank Borman.

Soviet cosmonaut Yuri Gagarin (left) shakes hands with NASA's *Gemini 4* astronauts Edward H. White II and James A. McDivitt at the Paris International Air Show in June 1965. Gagarin was the first human to orbit Earth, and White was the second to walk in space. Also shown are U.S. Vice President Hubert H. Humphrey (seated) and French premier Georges Pompidou (standing).

Shepard became the first American astronaut in space, aboard *Freedom 7*. And then, on February 20, 1962, John Glenn became the first American in orbit. In 4 hours and 55 minutes, he circled Earth three times aboard *Friendship 7*, and Americans had a new hero.

To meet President Kennedy's challenge, the National Aeronautics and Space Administration (NASA) went into high gear. First the Mercury, and then the Gemini, programs sent men into space, with astronauts orbiting Earth for longer and longer periods. With each mission, they learned more: how to function without gravity, how to spacewalk, how to fix equipment, and eventually, how to dock in space. Meanwhile, NASA also developed rockets powerful enough to reach the Moon. In order to orbit Earth, a spacecraft has to reach a speed of 18,000 miles (28,800 km) an hour; and in order to escape the gravity of Earth and get to the Moon, it has to reach a speed of 25,000 miles (40,300 km) per hour.

Astronaut Edwin "Buzz" Aldrin salutes the American flag on *Mare Tranquillitatis*. Because there is no atmosphere on the Moon, the flag had to be stiffened with a metal rod so it would appear to be waving in a breeze.

Neil Armstrong's footprint on the Moon. If no meteorite disturbs the moon dust, this footprint will last for millions of years.

In July 1964, *Ranger 7* made a planned crash on the Moon and transmitted photographs of the lunar surface. During the last 15 minutes of its flight, it sent back 4,316 pictures. In February 1966, the Russian *Luna 9* softlanded, proving that the dusty lunar surface was capable of supporting a lunar lander.

In 1967, NASA began the Apollo project, and in 1968, astronauts Frank Borman, Jim Lovell, and Bill Anders orbited the Moon 10 times in *Apollo 8*.

Finally, on July 16, 1969, *Apollo 11*'s Saturn rocket blasted off from the launch pad, carrying astronauts Neil Armstrong, Edwin "Buzz" Aldrin, and Michael Collins. Three days later, the lunar module, called the *Eagle*, separated from the command module and began its descent to the Moon. Its four legs landed on the surface at *Mare Tranquillitatis*, the Sea of Tranquility. Armstrong radioed back to mission control, "Houston, Tranquility Base here. The *Eagle* has landed."

On July 20, Neil Armstrong, dressed in a bulky spacesuit, opened the hatch and climbed down the ladder. For the first time, a human being put foot on the surface of the Moon. "That's one small step for man," Armstrong said, "one giant leap for mankind."

Aldrin joined him, and in about two and a half hours, they collected nearly 50 pounds (22.5 kg) of moon rocks and dust. Back on Earth, scientists analyzed the lunar material carefully after sterilizing it with ultraviolet light, peracetic acid, and sterile water, then

The Moon, Up Close and Personal

What does the Moon look like from ground level? After he returned to Earth, Neil Armstrong attempted to describe the view on the lunar surface:

> You generally have the impression of being on a desertlike surface, with rather light-colored hues. Yet when you look at the material from close range, as in your hand, you find that it's really charcoal gray. We had difficulties in perception of distance. For example . . . we had difficulty in guessing how far the hills on the horizon might be away from us. The peculiar phenomenon is the closeness of the horizon, due to the greater curvature of the Moon's surface—four times greater than on Earth; also it's an irregular surface, with crater rims overlying other crater rims.

Astronauts also found that it was hard to see the stars because of sunlight reflecting off the Moon rocks. (That's why, in photographs taken from the surface, the sky always looks black.) But when they shielded their eyes and got used to the dark, the stars suddenly appeared by the millions.

On July 24, 1969, command module of *Apollo 11* splashed down in the Pacific Ocean, just south of Hawaii. Shown here are the three astronauts in the life raft with a Navy frogman. They are wearing biological isolation garments and waiting for a helicopter to pick them up.

drying it in vacuum chambers filled with nitrogen so the rocks wouldn't disintegrate in Earth's atmosphere. To avoid contamination, scientists studying the rocks used long rubber gloves to reach into the vacuum chambers.

The first thing they discovered was that there had never been any life on the Moon. How could they know this? Because the rock contained no organic material at all, neither fossils of past life nor evidence of present life. There was no water in the rock. In one regard, the findings were a big relief. Now scientists could rest assured that the mission hadn't brought any alien germs from the Moon to Earth.

The next mission, *Apollo 12*, set up a scientific station on the *Oceanus Procellarum*, the Ocean of Storms. It included a seismometer to measure moonquakes and a machine to measure magnetic fields. The instruments continued to radio measurements back to Earth after the astronauts had left. The moonwalkers

Apollo 11 astronauts Neil Armstrong, Buzz Aldrin, and Michael Collins wave to the crowds during a ticker tape parade in New York City.

gathered 75 pounds (34 kg) of samples. When these were later analyzed, scientists noticed that their composition differed somewhat from that of the rocks gathered at *Mare Tranquillitatis*, demonstrating that it was important to land in as many different places as possible to get the most accurate information about the whole Moon.

On *Apollo 15, 16,* and *17,* astronauts were able to travel about the Moon in a Lunar Roving Vehicle, or moon buggy. Powered by 36-volt batteries, it went about 8 miles (13 km) per hour. On one of their explorations in a highland area called the Apennine Mountains, the astronauts of *Apollo 15* saw a rock that was perched on a mound of dirt and covered in white dust. When it was analyzed back on Earth, scientists found that it was more than four billion years old—almost as old as the Moon itself. Scientists later named it the Genesis rock.

In December 1972, the last Apollo mission, *Apollo 17,* landed on the edge of the Sea of Serenity. Its astronauts came upon an area of orange soil that later turned out to be composed of orange glass beads, which scientists believe erupted from lunar volcanoes some 3.5 billion years before.

Altogether, six Apollo missions brought back approximately 843 pounds (382 kg) of Moon rock and soil. Today, more than 30 years later, they are still being analyzed at the Johnson Space Center. Scientists there use isotopic analysis to determine the ages of the rocks. This technique is based on the rate at which radioactive atoms decay into other types of atoms.

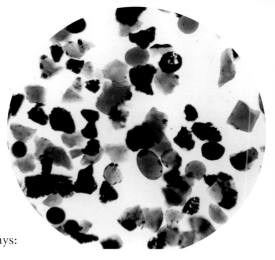

Apollo 17 astronaut Harrison J. Schmitt discovered an area of orange soil in Shorty Crater composed of these tiny orange and black beads. They were formed in volcanic "fire fountains" and sprayed onto the lunar surface.

Generally, scientists have discovered that Moon rock is very similar to Earth rock—with one important difference: Earth rock can form three ways: layers (sedimentary), by putting pressure on existing rock (metamorphic), or when magma cools (igneous). Moon rock is all igneous rock. Rocks from the light-colored highlands of the Moon, called "anorthosites," are the oldest rocks there. Like the Genesis rock, they are believed to have been formed during the Moon's birth, about 4.6 billion years ago. Anorthosites formed the first crust over the still red-hot, molten Moon.

Younger rocks, called basalts, formed when lava flowed over the maria about 3.6 billion years ago. These rocks are darker and heavier than the anorthosites. A third kind of rock, called breccia, resulted when meteors hit the lunar surface. The shattered meteors fused with melted moon crust to form these lumpy rocks.

The Apollo program ended in 1972, and as Eugene Cernan—to date, the last person to walk on the Moon—stepped back into the lunar module, he said, "God willing, we shall return with peace and hope for all mankind." His wish can still come true, because Moon exploration is not over. In February 1994, a new probe, *Clementine*, orbited the Moon for several months and sent back more than a million photographs. For the first time, we saw images that indicated what might be ice at the Moon's south pole. The crater there is so deep that sunlight cannot penetrate it, and temperatures remain bitterly cold. In 1998, the *Lunar Prospector* probe seemed to find ice at both poles, although more recent analysis has disputed this finding. If

Astronaut Jim Irwin sets up the first lunar roving vehicle during the *Apollo 15* mission, in the foothills of the lunar Apennine Mountains.

38

ice does exist, it is probably the remains of comets that impacted sometime in the distant past. Ice could—it is hoped—furnish water for a future Moon space station.

The Apollo missions gave us our first view of our home planet from a global perspective. Set against the backdrop of the Universe, Earth seems smaller and more fragile than we had imagined. But in the last 200 years, human activities have accelerated change around the globe. We have torn down forests, polluted the air, and dumped waste in the oceans. How has Earth as a whole responded to these environmental changes? What implications do these changes have for life in the future?

Advances in technology have given us the unprecedented opportunity to monitor the health of our planet. In the 1980s, scientists began to use data gathered on shuttle flights to study the land, vegetation, oceans, and atmosphere. Today, a fleet of satellites from NASA and its international partners helps scientists generate information about Earth. The Mission to Planet Earth (MTPE), the first craft of which was launched in 1991, is designed to track information about atmospheric ozone levels, forest fires and deforestation, earthquakes, hurricanes and other storms, volcanoes, and climate change.

The scope of the program is broad. The U.S./French oceanographic satellite *TOPEX/Poseidon*, for instance, measures wave height and average sea level. It has also been able to predict the El Niño phenomenon. Weather satellites can predict weather, such as upcoming hurricanes and other storms. Others satellites study solar radiation. Satellite laser radar (SLR) systems track the motion of Earth's tectonic plates. For example, they have tracked the island of Maui, Hawaii, which moves northwest toward Japan at three inches (7 cm) per year.

Previously, each satellite focused on only one aspect of Earth. In 1999, NASA launched the first complete Earth Observing System, designed to study Earth as a "complex series of interactions among life, water, and land." *Terra*, as the first satellite in the program is called, has already made the first global carbon monoxide measurements. For the first time, we'll be able to track air pollution across continents and oceans and to pinpoint the sources of climate changes. Someday the Earth Observing System might help us eliminate such pollution.

This false color map highlights the vast mineral deposits exposed on the surface of the Moon. If we ever return to the Moon to mine these minerals, maps like this will be of great importance.

40

Moon Gazing

Moon watching has always been a popular human activity. In a prehistoric mound tomb in Ireland, an intricate rock carving has been identified as a primitive map of the Moon. The first moon map discovered dates back to about 3000 B.C. Some 4,600 years later, scientist William Gilbert was credited with making the first naked-eye drawing of the Moon.

The Moon is still a great place for the amateur astronomer to explore, and it is possible to do it without magnification. Of course, one can see even better through a pair of binoculars or a small telescope.

All astronomical telescopes show upside-down images. For this reason, the image seen through a telescope will not be the same as the one seen through binoculars. Everything will be topsy-turvy—east will suddenly be west and vice versa. Because of this, astronomers disagree about which directions to use when referring to a lunar feature: those seen with the naked eye or viewed through a telescope. The directions given here are all in accordance with International Astronomical Union guidelines. They conform to the way the Moon looks when one gazes up into the sky.

Pick a clear night to begin moon watching. Bring a notebook, a pencil, a flashlight, a moon chart, and a pair of binoculars or a telescope. Before going out, use a circular pattern (such as an upside-down bowl) to draw a perfect circle in a notebook.

To get the most out of a Moon-gazing experience, follow its phases for a full month, checking every three to four days. (Find the phases on a Web site or use a regular calendar to determine the best time to start.) Contrary to popular belief, the full moon is not the best time to see all the features on the lunar surface. It's actually easier to make out craters and mountains during the crescent or half-moon phases, when they cast long, distinct shadows. The place where craters and mountains cast the sharpest shadows is at the terminator, the line where dark meets light.

By the way, don't expect to look up at the Moon and see the American flag waving in the middle of *Mare Tranquillitatis*. That would be like looking at Earth from space and expecting to see your house. Nothing the Apollo astronauts left on the Moon can be seen by any Earth-based telescope, no matter how powerful its magnification.

To be truly professional about moon gazing, record the time and date of each observation, the telescopic magnification, and the sky conditions. Although observations can begin at any time during the monthly cycle, it's most exciting to begin with the waxing crescent and watch the Moon "grow" and then diminish again. Just keep in mind that because the Moon rises about 50 minutes later every night, some of the phases might be in the middle of the night.

Waxing Crescent: The crescent moon becomes visible a few days after the new moon. At its thinnest, the whole unilluminated face of the Moon is seen—the "Old Moon in the New Moon's arms," as the old saying goes. The dark Moon is visible because of earthshine; that is, sunlight is reflected off the face of Earth and shines on the Moon.

The waxing crescent can be seen early in the evening just after sunset. As the crescent grows, one can see a large dark circle in the northeast. This is *Mare Crisium*, the Sea of Crises.

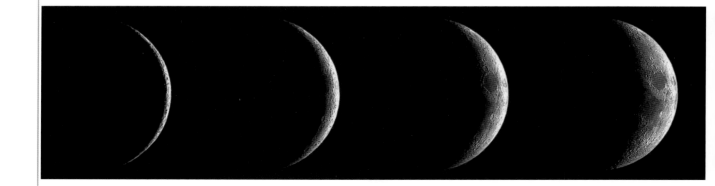

The First Quarter: A week after the new moon, the first-quarter moon becomes visible. It is sometimes referred to as the half-moon, because that is what it looks like. Now, just south of *Mare Crisium*, *Mare Fecunditatis* (Sea of Fertility) can be seen. To its northwest is the broad, flat shape of *Mare Tranquillitatis*. The imprint of Neil Armstrong's first footstep is located on its southern edge.

Waxing Gibbous: As the Moon continues to wax, some of its most dramatic features come into view. On the bright highlands in the Southern Hemisphere is the spectacular rayed crater Tycho. To its north, between the dark seas *Mare Nubium* (Sea of Clouds) and *Mare Imbrium* (Sea of Showers), is another rayed crater, Copernicus. A day or two later, it is joined by the rayed crater Kepler to the west.

Full Moon: Two weeks after the new moon, the full moon comes into brilliant view. In the fall, it rises at sunset a few nights in a row. This is the famed harvest moon, so called because it shines during the time of year when farmers harvest their crops. At full moon, most of the lunar features are flattened out in the glare of the Sun. Now the most massive sea on the Moon is apparent: *Oceanus Procellarum*, the Ocean of Storms. It stretches across an area more than half the size of the United States. Together with *Mare Imbrium* and *Mare Nubium*, it covers most of the Moon's Western Hemisphere.

Waning Gibbous: A few days later, the shadows begin creeping across the eastern half. The waning gibbous moon rises after sunset. Now is a good time to look for Clavius, just south of Tycho. One hundred forty-six miles (233 km) across, Clavius is one of the largest craters on the Moon, with an area greater than that of Switzerland. Because the Moon is now lighted from the other side, mountain ranges that were not readily apparent in the waxing gibbous become sharply clearer. Along the terminator, look for the Alps and the Apennines on the eastern edge of *Mare Imbrium*. (Mountain ranges on the Moon are often named after ones on Earth.)

Third Quarter: The third-quarter moon rises after midnight. This is a good time to look for the Jura Mountains above *Mare Imbrium*. As the terminator moves west, Grimaldi, a crater close to the western edge, might be visible

As night steals across its face, the waning crescent moon rises later and later into the early morning. Finally, it is overtaken by shadows and disappears into the darkness of space.

Further Information

Kerood, Robin. *The Earth*. Minneapolis, MN: Lerner Publications, 2000.

Kerrod, Robin. *The Moon*. Minneapolis, MN: Lerner Publications, 2000.

Ridpath, Ian. *Stars and Planets*. Eyewitness Handbooks. New York: DK Publishing, 1998.

Mitton, Simon and Jacqueline Mitton. *The Young Oxford Book of Astronomy*. New York: Oxford University Press, 1995.

Watters, Thomas R. *The Smithsonian Guide to the Planets*. New York: Macmillan, 1995.

NASA's images from its planetary exploration program
http://pds.jpl.nasa.gov/planets/welcome.htm

Odysseys Magazine's site for late-breaking news
http://www.odysseymagazine.com/pages/sci-encescoops.php

Science@NASA news home page (for all branches of astronomy and space science)
http://science.nasa.gov

Space.com home page http://www.space.com/

"The Nine Planets: A Multimedia Tour of the Solar System" home page
http://seds.lpl.arizona.edu/nineplanets/nineplanets/nineplanets.html

Glossary

atmosphere—The gaseous envelope that surrounds several of the planets and moons in our solar system.

continent—A large, unbroken landmass on Earth's surface.

core—The center, or middle, of an object. A planet's core is frequently hotter than its surface and under great pressure.

crust—The surface of a planet or moon where rock and mineral come in contact with an atmosphere or an ocean.

earthquake—A slip or jolt of Earth's crust that causes a wave of ground shifting and shaking.

eclipse—An astronomical event when one object either totally or partially blocks another object from view.

exosphere—The uppermost part of Earth's atmosphere, extending about 400 miles (650 km) from the planet's surface.

lithosphere—The outer, solid part of Earth's surface that includes the crust and parts of the upper mantle.

magnetic field—An area of magnetic influence that circulates between the two poles of a magnet.

magnetosphere—A magnetic field that envelopes Earth, flowing between the North Pole and the South Pole. The magnetosphere helps protect Earth from harmful cosmic influences.

mantle—Minerals that compose the inner layers of Earth.

magma—Molton rock.

mare—Latin word for *sea*. Used to describe dark, basalt-filled impact basins common on the face of the Moon visible from Earth.

meteor—A bright streak of light in the sky caused by the entry into Earth's atmosphere of a meteoroid.

meteorite—A meteoroid that reaches the surface of a planet or moon without being completely vaporized.

meteoroid—A small, solid body in the solar system outside Earth's atmosphere.

mesosphere—A band of Earth's atmosphere that extends about 53 miles (85 km) from its surface. Here temperatures begin to drop.

ozone—A rare molecule made of three oxygen atoms that forms a protective layer high in Earth's atmosphere.

plate tectonics—The movement of great slabs of Earth's crust that can cause earthquakes and volcanic eruptions.

solar wind—A continuous stream of charged particles that are released from the Sun and hurled outward into space at speeds up to 500 miles (800 km) per second.

stratosphere—A layer of Earth's atmosphere that lies above the troposphere and reaches to about 31 miles (50 km) high. It holds the protective ozone layer.

terrestrial planet—One of the four rocky, or inner, planets in the solar system.

tidal force—The gravitational pull on planetary objects from nearby planets and moons.

thermosphere—The upper layer of Earth's atmosphere. The thermosphere extends about 300 miles (480 km) from Earth's surface.

troposphere—The layer of atmosphere closest to Earth, where the breathable air comes from and where weather takes place. It stretches from the ground about 5 to12 miles (8–18 km) high.

volcano—A bulge or mountain in a planet's surface caused by pressure from the ground beneath it.

wane—To slowly lose brightness or vitality. When the Moon moves from full and begins to become smaller, it is called a waning moon.

wax—To slowly gain brightness or vitality. When the Moon moves from a sliver to its full state, it is called a waxing moon.

Index